Poetic Word

of the Day
for Presidential Candidates

(In other words "How to Keep a President In Line")
(In other words "How to Pick a President")

A booklet of political observations and remedies proposed by an amateur poet. Principals of political character; good for every era, every election.

Preface and Author's Notes

We all know that there's something wrong in our politics today. Here's a booklet that just might help us to better understand, and maybe even come closer to fixing, our politics.

Some of us are looking for the basics. This is a small booklet of presidential and political principles that we can use. Then, we regular, normal people (who are not politicians) can keep the

President **_IN LINE_** without defaulting to the media to do the job. This is a framework rather than a specific procedure. It is not suggestions for congressional acts and such. This is a framework of 64 principles; *"ma and pa"* ideals of the American society; much desired qualities. The format is similar to the **Boy Scout Law** in that it is a list of desirable qualities in a human being. The Boy Scout Law is a list of 12 desirable qualities in boys. This booklet lists 64 qualities for adult men and women. It's applied poetry with some applied philosophy thrown in. It's not intended to be totally comprehensive and all-inclusive.

This booklet is a call to action! ... A call to action for our citizenship to never be fooled again! With these presidential and political principles, I believe we can hold our politicians accountable in a way that we can all easily understand. For example, taken from the text we can ask: Is he *DIPLOMATIC*? Is he *KINDLY*? Can he *SIFT* effectively? Does he know that the *SKY* is the limit to our abilities and our dreams? Does he get the picture and really realize how incredibly *FAR* the Secretary of State must travel when he visits so many distant foreign countries?

This booklet is a surface-level examination of the state of affairs of this day and age and of this nation, its political problems and how they relate to these simple one-word remedies and one-word observations.

One-word observations! ... That's what this is ... one word at a time, one principle at a time to hold up next to our politicians. It's the start of looking more deeply. By these principles we can all judge and evaluate whether or not a particular candidate measures up. YES!--We can do this simply by asking whether or not our presidential candidates can live up to these powerful, commanding little words. These simple poetic words can help us evaluate our political candidates in a way that everyone can understand.

We use ONE WORD AT A TIME SO EVERYONE CAN CLEARLY UNDERSTAND. I know (yes, we all know) that one of the last things we Americans need is any lecturing. So, I'm very sorry, it is true -- this is a literary disguise for a little bit of lecturing. Perhaps you should accept this small amount of lecturing, and then let's get on with fixing our broken politics. Do you have a better plan? My editor informs me that this booklet is called "editorial prose."

BEWARE! BEWARE!! There may be some people and some organizations in the United States who have it in their personal and business interests for the general public and the common man to remain confused. BEWARE!

Who is this booklet for? This booklet is for all Americans: rich or poor; intelligent or not; political or non-political; inclined toward poetry or not so inclined. This booklet is for all Americans who are looking for our nation to get better -- get better fast and stay that way for hundreds of years into the future.

This booklet has a few good, solid concepts. It is also likely that it has some run-on concepts that are obvious and may be considered a filler to some of you. I am sorry if you think that it's not infinitely interesting and, perhaps, not absolutely perfect and eloquent and succinct.

This booklet was created during the election year 2008 when George W. Bush was still the President of the United States. References are made to him and to the major candidates for election year 2008.

When referring to the President, the words "he," "his," and "Mr." are used. This is for the purposes of uniformity and ease of reading; it is not intended as gender bias.

Notes to the Reader: These words are **representational**. The reader is expected to "fill in the blanks," read between the lines; read between the words of the day and expand the meaning as he/she sees fit to make more sense in his/her own life.

I truly wish every word and every phrase in this booklet were precisely refined, were exactly and perfectly applicable, and would come to an extremely important point time and time again. Though I have worked hard to refine this as much as possible, I admit there are many places where you will have to read on and not expect perfection.

Notes about the Author

Paul Christopher Anzalone, is, to a large extent, a functioning schizophrenic. If I wasn't a schizophrenic, I may have finished this booklet much sooner when that election cycle was taking place. That said, it seems there is still an element of ongoing and current relevance here, and this booklet is still applicable today ... nine years later. It is relevant for the future too, as long as our current industrial and urban society lives on. In my defense for taking so long to publish this booklet, I can say that I needed to live with these words for a long time to gauge the merit and longevity and effectiveness of this overall idea of Poetic Words for Presidential Candidates to determine if this work might help us over the long run. One detracting aspect of my observations of American and international affairs is that this booklet probably looks at the issues and poetic words of the day and the ideas they present in a *simplistic* way. However, it is just a surface level beginning, as I stated previously.

My views are not always going to be politically correct (for example, when I speak about gay people and their lifestyles). It is not my intention to offend anyone, but this work does express my own personal viewpoints and what I believe to be true and what I understand to be biblical.

Dictionaries and Thesauruses ... There may be people who do not like dictionaries but, as my grandmother Margarita Flynn would tell me, "Look it up!" She would say, "If you come to a word that you don't know the meaning of, then look it up!" Oftentimes, we come to a word for which we do not know the meaning. If we pass by and keep reading, it's likely we are going to miss out on the meaning of that sentence and there will be confusion and misunderstanding to follow.   So, take my grandmother's advice and look up the words you do not know. You will be a happier reader and you'll gain more in life.

I like the popular song "Big Shot" by Billy Joel. I'm not trying to be a "big shot" and get a book published. I'm just trying to **give back** to people some of the knowledge and experience that have been judiciously bestowed upon me over the years.

Poetic Word of the Day for Presidential Candidates

Sunday, June 29, 2008

Poetic Word of the Day for Presidential Candidates: **GENERIC**

Too bad a President has to be GENERIC ... bland and rather boring; regular, like corn flakes and oatmeal. That's one stretch of the definition for the word GENERIC.

How come? because he must be liked by so many people. It seems this leaves little room for thoughtful or beautiful, rugged nor independent poetry. Too bad his performance as President can't be an eight-year graceful poem. I have purposely stated "eight" years as I believe that our political calendar is much too short and that most U.S. Presidents should serve for at least eight years in one term; then have an election to see if they should serve another four-year term. (It's because our election season is far too long and is excruciatingly painful.)

Monday, June 30, 2008

Poetic Word of the Day for Presidential Candidates: **ALTRUISM**

Let's get right down to it. Dear readers and all concerned citizens: You had better learn what the word *ALTRUISM* means. Politics is a job. They (the politicians) must eat, pay bills, pay for a house, and send the kids to college -- just like anybody. That's the simple reason that most of them are politicians ... they need a job like everyone else. They need money. This is not a very altruistic reason to be in politics. I repeat, this is not a very altruistic reason to be in politics.

ALTRUISM is one of the best and most important reasons for a person to be considering politics. ALTRUISM is a great big lofty ideal. Unfortunately, politicians are not normally known for their ALTRUISM. Do some studying on the concept of ALTRUISM.

For most of us *money* is the tool that acts as our main motivator. In short, it's plain old common sense for a person to try to get the highest paying job that he/she can. This will not work for politics. Unfortunately, money is not the best motivator in cases where a nation and its people need to have their overall best interests looked after. ALTRUISM must be involved. ALTRUISM is where we do good in the world, with or without the motivation of money. People everywhere try to obtain large amounts of money, but money, as such, is an insufficient motivator where the massive, overall good must be the priority -- the priority of the President.

Money, it seems, will not always be the put-things-into-motion perfect motivator that we think it should be. Time and money seem like the right things; they seem like a direct way of looking at life. Yet now, the way things are, we have to pose questions about this usually effective motivator. More money is not the answer. ALTRUISM may be the magical force that picks up where money alone cannot do the job.

Tuesday, July 1, 2008

Poetic Word of the Day for Presidential Candidates: **THOROUGH**

A President should check things out! Check under the rocks. Check under the manhole covers. Check in the soldiers' trenches. Check in the workers' tool boxes. Check in the students' lockers -- there might be some good advice in there next to the marijuana and gym shorts. As we all know, our youth can give us some good advice too. (We are not condoning the use of marijuana but we realize that it is common). We ask our President to make the best decisions and to avoid overlooking important aspects. We ask the President to check things out and be THOROUGH.   This concept is obvious and it's what we expect!

Wednesday, July 2, 2008

Poetic Word of the Day for Presidential Candidates: **THINK**

A presidential candidate should give plenty of time to thinking. Quick decisions are okay on very obvious matters; however, the deep, multifaceted problems a President can, and will, face require a person who knows how to spend time alone thinking.

A President should be able to use *Speed THINK* when necessary! *Speed THINK* is a very important skill for a presidential candidate. We should consider this: It is necessary to *Speed THINK* in order to sort out and consider many facets of a question or problem, especially when time is short and a decision must be made quickly. Of course, there are also other, new questions coming soon, so the ability to *Speed THINK* would be a very valuable tool for a President.

We ask a President to do the obvious and THINK so we don't sink. One cannot THINK if one is running one's mouth all of the time.

Thursday, July 3, 2008

Poetic Word of the Day for Presidential Candidates: **GROUNDED**

A presidential candidate should be one who has <u>not always had the fortunate life.</u> He has learned the value of hard work and, sometimes, adversity.   He knows how to get his hands and shoes dirty without complaining. He knows how to be one of the struggling people (even though, if elected, he will get royal treatment for the rest of his life).

He knows how to bow his head, like with a little head nod to others, or to God the Father Almighty, or to the evolution god, -- not that I believe in the evolution god -- or to anybody because he has made human mistakes and will make them again.

Because he is a performer (and all of his performances are not flawless), humility can be shown with a head nod or bow. A good example of this is Johnny Cash. I noticed on public television that Johnny Cash bowed (a noticeable little head nod). He's a very recognized figure, and he's bowing while he walks into the prison to perform. This gesture shows that he's human, not perfect, and that he knows you see him.

You don't have to bow to anyone, really, but I bow because of the human problems I have been through in my life. I can remember once, an old man bowing (head nod) just as he was walking from the parking lot into the store and I thought to myself, "How come he's doing that? I see no reason." Now that I've lived so many more years and have seen more of what nature and the world has done to me (and everyone), I realize that bowing, or a slight head nod, is not such a bad thing. There may be people who think that bowing is dumb. Maybe life will treat them better. They deserve a big chance to do life right … and never have to bow.

GROUNDED also means there's some common sense in there somewhere. Common sense means knowing how much to talk because, oftentimes, too much talking confuses the public and, heaven forbid, even *bores* the public. Common sense. Now, couldn't we write a whole book about common sense? Gardeners, machinists, farmers and cattlemen, veterinarians, shoe repair people, construction workers, auto mechanics, math and science teachers, kindly old gentlemen, bicycle repair people - these are some of the people we turn to for common sense. Unfortunately, our Presidents are not usually known for their nitty-gritty common sense.

There's much more to say about being GROUNDED. We might need a GROUNDED, Part 2; but, for now, we go on.

Friday, July 4, 2008

Poetic Word of the Day for Presidential Candidates: **FAMILY**

Enough cannot be said about the word FAMILY. The power, presence, influence, and needs of FAMILY can never be underestimated. A presidential candidate should ideally be a person who has a wife and children, so he intimately knows the joys, sorrows, problems, and triumphs that come with the core unit of American life. Remember, please, dear reader, that moms and dads must pay out a great deal of money to raise a FAMILY. Therefore, money (the idea of money and the actuality of money as a tool) is very important to the FAMILY unit. Please remember that raising a FAMILY is expensive and college is expensive. There are many, many reasons why we want to emphasize that the *FAMILY unit* in our nation is extremely important -- much more than just a passing word can bring. (Let's not forget our single people. Sometimes, it's very hard to be single).

Saturday, July 5, 2008

Poetic Word of the Day for Presidential Candidates: **REVERENT**

Personally, I believe in Yahweh and Jesus Christ His only Son, and I make God a part of my everyday life. Yes, I believe that organized religion is, and can be, an important and essential part of this massive, overall good that we are working to achieve.

We -- those of us who have studied Judeo-Christian viewpoints-- would like to apologize to atheists and gay people. We value you as people, but we definitely object to your lifestyle. We are sorry that we don't know how to include your values when they are so deeply against Yahweh's rules. We like people. We like gay people too, but we just don't agree with your lifestyle. Yahweh has clearly spoken out against the gay lifestyle in his book. Two of those verses are located in The Book of Leviticus, Chapter 18, Verse 22, and The Acts of the Apostles, Chapter 15, Verse 29. There are a few others.

Another thought I have about the gay lifestyle is that they should find a different symbol besides the rainbow of colors. The rainbow of colors is for children to marvel at, not for gays to get "hooked up." I'm sorry, but doesn't that just strike you as wrong? It may be that gay people are using the rainbow to lure our young with a pretty rainbow of colors. Most likely, they have this in their future agenda ... Sex for everybody and with anybody. Let's try to stop it right here.

This country was founded on the values of Christianity. If you make a list of all this country's founding fathers and keep track of how many were devout Christians, you will see this to be true. Now, we've expanded our society to accept *all* religions in the USA. We even allow and respect those who choose NO religion (atheists) or those who believe in nature as God (pantheists). We cannot ignore our advances in science, but it seems to me--and it's completely real to me--that there is an eternal God named Yahweh or Jehovah. The words "Yahweh" and "Jehovah" actually mean *"the cause to be."* Do we know if God chose his own name? That's a good question for those of us who read the Bible.

Can we answer the ultimate question? "Is there really an all-powerful God who has a personality and requests humans to do His will?" Once, while in public, in a particular circumstance, a wise old woman said very loudly: "FEAR GOD! **FEAR GOD!**" We probably cannot absolutely, in human and earthly understanding, actually answer the question, "Is there really an all-powerful God?" We will find out at our death, or at Jesus' second coming. Can I tell you that there are a few authors who have claimed to have *proved* the existence of God, the Father Almighty, in books and technical and scholarly papers?

Our money spells out "In God We Trust." In human terms, faith is nearly all we have, plus the Bible and the history of Jesus' life on earth. We'd be wise to be REVERENT. There's really no place in modern life without God the Father Almighty as a part of our every day. That's my deeply held opinion and belief.

Karl Marx said "Religion is the opiate of the masses ...." I believe he was wrong. For people who are non-believers, my opinion is that Yahweh is ... at the very minimum that we can agree upon without too much discussion and explanation ... *the force of the unknown*. Surely, you acknowledge there is plenty of unknown force in this universe. One way to explain it is that this means there is a God.   We can have these discussions as we find it more clearly spelled out; and maybe we can really work, we poets, to find it more clearly spelled out.

Sunday, July 6, 2008

Poetic Word of the Day for Presidential Candidates: **CONNECTOR**

A presidential candidate should have the obvious qualities of being an excellent socializer and people/idea CONNECTOR.

Most of the people talented in this capacity are very good at connecting people and ideas. In our minds we can conjecture that being a CONNECTOR is one thing, but having the itinerary, plan, program, and vision well-defined in the leader's mind is what we need. Then, we'll bet the leader is a good CONNECTOR as well (or maybe he can hire a good CONNECTOR).

It doesn't seem that anything is really going to change in Washington, DC. The "establishment", as it is called, is very well-entrenched. Therefore, we can begin to ask the questions: "How do we systematically, in a measured way, take apart the establishment? Is it even necessary to do so?" This is not a revolution, but rather a measured and planned effort toward a vision.

We know that most politicians and other government employees are just people trying to do their best. Unfortunately, as we grow in wisdom, we find that there are some who intentionally try to cheat us, or take advantage of us, when we aren't looking or are not able to keep tabs on the whole political and congressional thing. Being a CONNECTOR is a necessary, yet very difficult, task in our political system. There's nothing wrong with a slow and thorough process of reform on certain kinds of tasks and issues. Knowing how Washington works is helpful, but working for the public and not for the special interest groups is just as important.

Remember, a CONNECTOR is also an important piece of putting things together. This is clearly seen when defined in terms of plumbing, electrical, mechanical, and even in carpentry work. All of these trades have a device or object that they use called a CONNECTOR. This necessary device is used to make their jobs easier … to join two parts together. This is significant.

Monday, July 7, 2008

Poetic Word of the Day for Presidential Candidates: **COURAGEOUS**

The job of President probably requires the most courage of any human being in this country. For one thing, it seems that it is more COURAGEOUS to prevent war than it is to start one.

This characteristic may seem obvious; however, it takes more courage to seek and portray the truth than most people are willing to allow. There are many extreme positions on numerous issues. Doesn't it take courage to listen to and examine a position that is opposite from your own? Doesn't it take courage to judge and make decisions that people on one side or the other will find disagreeable?

One of our most highly regarded former Presidents, John Fitzgerald Kennedy wrote a book titled <u>Profiles in Courage</u>. Let's read it!

Tuesday, July 08, 2008

Poetic Word of the Day for Presidential Candidates: **COFFEE**

COFFEE is a one-of-a-kind word. No one can top COFFEE for an ideal. COFFEE is a luxury, and the idea of *having COFFEE* is about fostering people getting together for friendship, early in the morning (or anytime of the day).

The non-COFFEE drinkers aren't going to like this much, but the principle is this: Find an excuse to like COFFEE (or pretend to like it) to share time with others! Share time with co-workers, family, or absolutely any citizen if you are a presidential candidate. The conversation doesn't always have to be on current events or the most recent crisis. The conversation can be on our hopes and dreams and destinations as a nation ... like: How far will we ever make it out into space?

When we share time with others, we can know what others know. Who knows? A little COFFEE today might prevent a fuel crisis tomorrow. Presidential candidates should know and practice the principle of COFFEE.

Wednesday, July 09, 2008

Poetic Word of the Day for Presidential Candidates: **CRISIS**

This is one of the President's main jobs: CRISIS preventer. A President is the person who will work to prevent a CRISIS from developing and will come to our aid immediately when a CRISIS happens.

This list of presidential principles is generally not in a hierarchical order, but let's pose this question: "How come the principle of COFFEE comes before the principle of CRISIS?" If the President does his coffee right, then most crises can be avoided!

We have natural disaster crises, and we have all kinds of other crises. Therefore, the President will be a CRISIS manager. It seems the best way to manage a CRISIS is to work to avoid it a long time before it happens. We call that being "proactive!"

Thursday, July 10, 2008

Poetic Word of the Day for Presidential Candidates: **CROWD**

A presidential candidate should be comfortable in all kinds of crowds. We can think of many different types of crowds: TV CROWD, Gun CROWD, Small CROWD, Coffee CROWD, Outspoken CROWD, CROWD that needs no help, CROWD that needs help, Hurting CROWD, Horse CROWD, Car CROWD, Train CROWD, Weapons CROWD, Jesus CROWD, the Lonely CROWD, Indoor CROWD, Outdoor CROWD, Indoor/Outdoor CROWD, Financial CROWD, Fusion CROWD, Dinner CROWD, Street CROWD, Game Day CROWD, Tailgate CROWD, China CROWD, Construction CROWD, Manufacturing CROWD, Studious CROWD, Scientific CROWD, Sociology CROWD, Space CROWD, NASA CROWD, Political CROWD, ESPN CROWD, Run with the CROWD, the CROWD he runs with, "Face in the CROWD," (a song by the Hi-Lo's jazz vocal quartet).

Here are some other words and phrases similar to CROWD:

Folks, Intuitive, Population, Social Interaction, Social Psychology, Rat Race, Social, Social Worker, Social Security, Social Government Agency, Civic, Small Town, City, City Planners, Slum, Traffic Congestion, American Sociological Association, Pack (as in wolves), Pride (as in lions), "People," (a song by Barbara Streisand), Group, Gang, Sociologist.

The Poetic Word of the Day for Presidential Candidates is not "Sociologist." This is a good word, but not a very good poetic word. It is CROWD.

Friday, July 11, 2008

Poetic Word of the Day for Presidential Candidates: **QUARRY**

How come QUARRY? For what reason is this today's word? QUARRY is the source--of the infrastructure. Put the QUARRY together with the Crowd and with science and machines, and we then have our infrastructure.

It seems to me that a QUARRY would be an extremely boring place. We must remember there are people in a QUARRY along with the raw materials, and these people have to find a way to keep going and stay motivated to make it fun and efficient. This is America NOW.

And, perhaps, the operators at the QUARRY are in a drilling machine or operating other machinery all day by themselves. Hopefully, they still get 15-minute breaks and a half hour for lunch. At least they have the radio to keep them company all day. Maybe that's enough for now.

QUARRY is also a symbolic word worthy of thought and examination. It exemplifies how lonely people (in terms of no one else around) get through the long days. A QUARRY worker could be one very bored worker. Yes, it is boring work but we need these people. You might consider becoming a QUARRY worker yourself! We'll find you some glory to gain from it.

Saturday, July 12, 2008

Poetic Word of the Day for Presidential Candidates: **TALE**

Wouldn't it be great if our candidates could tell a long story instead of the same old speech? And wouldn't it be great if our President could always have a long anecdote just right for the occasion? He would be a comfortable, grandfather-like person. We would sit on his lap and he'd never lead us astray. How we can wish!

Here is a challenge to the speech writers: Give us some stories please! Fact or fiction, a good story will take us away from our economic and health problems. However, keep the QUARRY in the mix because we need all the long, hard work in there too. We don't have to rely only on TV and movies and novels to always do that, now do we? How about a President who can tell a good TALE?

It takes imagination and vision to be a good TALE-telling President. This is a very desirable quality in a President.

Sunday, July 13, 2008

Poetic Word of the Day for Presidential Candidates: **SHERIFF**

Perhaps we need to slow down a bit with the hard-hitting words and find a few not-so-obvious words for our candidates, like SHERIFF.

Supporting your local police force is an obvious, regular kind of duty for the President. Presidential candidates must be concerned about police stuff. Otherwise, there would be chaos.

So today's word could also be many other similar words like "cop," or "Scotland Yard," or "FBI," or "guard," or "traffic cop," or "gun," or "sniper," ... or SHERIFF, That's it! It's SHERIFF!

"Constable" is another word similar to SHERIFF, but "Constable" is for the future. There is a fine line of a difference between the meanings of SHERIFF and "Constable." I think the word "Constable" is something to look forward to in the future as we, perhaps, become more like the country of England and do not need gun-toting crime fighters, as such, but rather peacekeepers on the street. From a distance, at one time, it seemed that England was more civilized in this area. Andy Griffith was kind of a constable, wasn't he? Now we can all go and watch a few reruns of *Mayberry RFD*.

Monday, July 14, 2008

Poetic Word of the Day for Presidential Candidates: **ATHLETE**

Most of us know about athletes. Many of us admire professional athletes. They inspire us and give us our national pastimes. As well, we remember the baseball and football backyard, side-yard, and front-street games we played when we were kids. We loved that. Being coordinated also has something to do with it. The President should be coordinated and active and also respect the physical aspect of life, even if the President isn't so physical himself. Plus, since sporting events seem to dominate our weekends, we adults should give *all of Sunday* back to Yahweh.

Tuesday, July 15, 2008

Poetic Word of the Day for Presidential Candidates: **FAST**

Politicians and Presidents should be FAST at something, be it sports or brainpower. They were, and are, FAST at something (hopefully, not just FAST at making money) and they gained some respect for it. Being FAST at something is important.

Wednesday, July 16, 2008

Poetic Word of the Day for Presidential Candidates: **ACCEPT**

The presidential candidates should ACCEPT themselves--good and bad, past, present, and future. They should also ACCEPT all of us, as citizens, just as we are and as we could be.

We might ACCEPT the current state of affairs of our country, even though it's far from perfect, yet still remember that we are boundless with creativity and answers that will solve our problems.

To ACCEPT is really about oneself, whether you are a presidential candidate or just a regular citizen. It is about finding yourself to be okay, even when there may be some undesirable stuff, and it's about finding what it takes inside to make things better.

It's also about accepting your spouse, as you slowly discover that your marriage may not be the storybook marriage you thought it would be. Even so, don't get a divorce. Divorce only adds to our national problems.

You should ACCEPT yourself, good and bad. ACCEPT who you are as a person with the human limitations that we all have, and also ACCEPT others for who they are and who they could be.

The presidential candidates should ACCEPT and know themselves. They should ACCEPT the citizens the way they are right now. Improvement can always come.

We should ACCEPT the current state of affairs, knowing, believing, and inspiring the nation, and ourselves, to take the necessary steps toward a better vision for the future.

Do we ACCEPT that the President is the greatest person in America at a certain time? He may not be the greatest, yet somehow we think he is. His tone (not just the tone of his voice) is the tone of the future. His tone should inspire us to realize our group goals and individual dreams.

Thursday, July 17, 2008

Poetic Word of the Day for Presidential Candidates: **GARDEN**

Not every family has a GARDEN, but a GARDEN can help your family get away from the "rat race." It can also give your family some good, healthy food!

Friday, July 18, 2008

Poetic Word of the Day for Presidential Candidates: **WHEELS**

The USA has lots of WHEELS, and we would like to keep our WHEELS rolling. We may have to slow down for a while to re-evaluate, but there is endless, clean energy out there somewhere to drive our WHEELS, our industries, and our other stuff. We also should be mindful of our *WHEELS* way of life that is so dependent upon fossil fuels. U.S. citizens generate far more, on average, in greenhouse gasses than other world citizens. It's truly not right for the USA to pollute the air with these overly high amounts (in proportion) of greenhouse gasses. The last I read the USA was the greatest air polluter.

Saturday, July 19, 2008

Poetic Word of the Day for Presidential Candidates: **AWARE**

To be deeply AWARE and have a widespread, grounded and thorough awareness is not easy for a presidential candidate, but we expect it. It's been said before: This is why it is truly lunacy for a person to consider running for the Presidency. In other words, I'm suggesting here that a President is actually somewhat detached from real life, maybe to the point of having a shrouded or even foggy life, or perhaps to the point of some kind of actual lunacy. Maybe we change the President's job description and salvage what we can in our nation (not to be pessimistic). Some think that the country is too big for one President and if he makes some mistakes, the ripple effect will negatively impact too many people. However, this is one of the risks of life. We need and want strong leaders, but we are cautious about how much power we give them.

We can't change the presidential candidates. Either they are AWARE, or they are not.

"Awareness" is a big word, and it might drive a presidential candidate crazy to consider all of the awareness he must have. A presidential candidate might never get eight hours of sleep. If he does, then we might say he is not doing his job.

We are sure our presidential candidates are AWARE of what's going on, to a large degree. Obviously, they know there are drugs on the streets, murders, rapes, wars, etc. Hopefully, they also know that there are millions of people who are trying really hard to live a decent, good life. We ask the Washington establishment to be AWARE of our good efforts too. They probably don't care.

Being both AWARE and thorough are important qualities for our presidential candidates. AWARE and "Thorough" go hand in hand.

Awareness goes deep. Conjecture is one thing, but seeing and knowing from firsthand observation--well, there's nothing that can replace that kind of awareness. Much of the information a person will get when he is President will be from his advisors. That's not firsthand knowledge. (It is possible to create a world where the spy will have a job, but he will be so bored because now there will be a current, relative time of peace.)

I'm not trying to separate the good people from the bad people. That's for God the Father Almighty to do, so we really shouldn't try … except for the obvious. "Freedom" has a very wide definition here, and we don't want to use the "J word" (Justice). It's just too vague and impractical to use in everyday poetic language. Yes, the word "Justice" can be applied to individual cases. But, please, let's not get bogged down with the word "Justice" right now. We have many qualified judges and a distinguished and competent court and judicial system. We will let them handle that difficult task before them.

Sunday, July 20, 2008

Poetic Word of the Day for Presidential Candidates: **FABRIC**

FABRIC is a good word to follow "Aware." What is the FABRIC of America today? What are Americans made of? A book I remember of the late 1970s was about what Americans did for their work. (I'm sorry, I've searched for the title and I haven't been able to find it). Another similar book could be written for today's society of the 2010's and the 2020's. What is the current research about America in the area of work and contentment?

For example, how many are in the full-time work force? How many are in the part-time work force? How many are in manufacturing? How many are in raw materials? How many are in the service industries? How many are doing blueprints and other paperwork? How many work in the livestock industry? How many work in farm commodities? How many work in growing nuts, fruits, and vegetables? And, how many of these workers consider themselves to be <u>content</u>?

Shall we learn about how contented and happy we are with our work and whether or not we believe some change is necessary?

Of course, we'd like to know about the FABRIC that the President is cut from as well. We want to know what kind of hard work he does. Is it just shuffling things around, or does he make things happen? Does he have solid skills? "Skills"--now that is a key word. A President's FABRIC is made up of his skills, not just *who* he knows.   Does he know how to type? Can he navigate around word processing and spreadsheet software?

We need a national vision, and we also need the follow-through to get us to that vision. (President Obama is not the first to say that we should have a man on Mars by 2030.) It's more than just taking care of ourselves. Of course, taking care of our aging population is high on the list. But, that's not the end and final destination of all of our efforts. Vision and follow-through will get us through our problems. Let's see what these presidential candidates can share about their FABRIC to create our collective vision and take action to make something of our nation. We need some kind of national goal, I think. Yes, some kind of national goal . . . .

Another Day ...

Poetic Word of the Day for Presidential Candidates: **MEASURED CHANGE**

This is the first two-word poetic word of the day. *It is that important.* When President Obama was a candidate, he spoke of *"change"* in Washington. But, I think it was just a slogan to get him elected. I don't think he would really know how to change the establishment in Washington.   It is too well-entrenched, so it is unlikely to change. There would be battles that would stall and go nowhere (and, they did).

So, the next President might propose a MEASURED CHANGE approach that is slight and try to work with those kinds of methods. Somebody has probably already had this idea. I'm not a Washington insider, and I don't really follow all Washington politics, just the major issues. As citizens, we can state, or perhaps dictate, where we think a President might start this kind of change process.   This is important--yes, MEASURED CHANGE!

Monday, July 21, 2008

Poetic Word of the Day for Presidential Candidates: **FAR**

The politicians and candidates seem so FAR away. I'm not trying to be pessimistic, but it seems like they're not really going to make things right. So, most of the time, we just ignore them. That's important: *Most of the time we just ignore them.* It's sad, but very true.

Tuesday, July 22, 2008

Poetic Word of the Day for Presidential Candidates: **PRETEND**

Let's PRETEND there's a movie out there that has a message: a message that can last a lifetime, a message that will make us chuckle over and over, a message that will end abortion, a message that will do the housework.

Let's PRETEND there's a trucker out there who can haul freight. This trucker hauls the biggest load and his truck goes the fastest, even in the mountains. He forged his own wheels and custom-built his own truck.

When we use the word PRETEND we have to be very cautious. It's great for kids (and for adults too) to watch movies. But, we should be cautious and make sure we don't mix up fiction with reality and then fabricate an impossible illusion. So, PRETEND is a fantasy and fiction word that is applicable to certain things. Let's both pray and use our intelligence to know when it's acceptable to use the word PRETEND.

Another Day ...

Poetic Word of the Day for Presidential Candidates: **SALVAGE**

SALVAGE can be both a verb and a noun.

Remember, one person's junk is another person's treasure. Believe it or not, it seems to me that we are trying to SALVAGE this country.

It seems to me we can handle more population if we're all not driving on the same streets at exactly the same time. It seems to me that the original government framework may not have been meant for 300 million people.

The problems in our country are really, really bad. I have picked up on the politicians' frequently used word "Reform." Reform is necessary and there must be measured change. It seems like there is a lot of bickering so, please, once we get our new President, let's see if incremental legislation can get us started on the right foot. We need effort in a positive direction, no matter how small.

Not being a Washington insider, I don't really know the problems that the politicians think are the most important. But, I believe that the future of Social Security and U.S. manufacturing are definitely problem areas.

You can probably guess my stand on abortion. Ending abortion does not have to be the job of the government. Society and communities and TV (maybe even McDonald's) can very strongly plant the idea of avoiding abortion in our young people's minds. Legal or not, we do not want any abortions. Can't we provide some corrective, positive reinforcement to fight this terrible national problem?

Wednesday, July 23, 2008

Poetic Word of the Day for Presidential Candidates: **ACTUATOR**

ACTUATOR ... as in nuts and bolts and gears and conveyors and vacuum packaging and controllers and actuators ... as in: "the numbing sounds of the factory ..."

Thursday, July 24, 2008

Poetic Word of the Day for Presidential Candidates: **AQUIFER**

There are water battles in the western parts of the country. Even Kansas may have issues with their AQUIFER. According to the media, the water situation is serious. The water issue is one of our most pressing problems today. As I understand it, desalinization plants can solve this issue. However, desalinization plants use huge amounts of energy. Thus, it seems like, once again, it's *clean energy* to the rescue. It's clean energy that will rescue us from our water problems. A great President will guide us through these water and energy issues and will make the correct decisions.

Friday, July 25, 2008

Poetic Word of the Day for Presidential Candidates: **ALPINE**

For some reason we are all still trying to escape and pretend--to get away to the ALPINE snow and become a ski bum. Anybody could be a ski bum. A ski bum gets to ski all day. Ski bums don't know what's for dinner. It's okay when we are young, in our teenage years and in our twenties, but not as responsible adults.

Saturday, July 26, 2008

Poetic Word of the Day for Presidential Candidates: **ROLLERS**

ROLLERS are in pulleys and free-moving wheels. Stainless ROLLERS are pretty to look at, and they roll freely. But, let's not forget that some force (clean energy once again) is necessary to make them move.

Sunday, July 27, 2008

Poetic Word of the Day for Presidential Candidates: **KINDLY**

KINDLY as in a "KINDLY Old Man." A KINDLY old man can help you with practically anything. Is there a KINDLY old man who can tell us how old people made it when there was no Social Security? Is there a KINDLY old man who can tell us how we can make it when we reach some kind of unmovable, unbending wall? For example, a problem with a supervisor that seems like it has no solution?

Monday, July 28, 2008

Poetic Word of the Day for Presidential Candidates: **MICROMETER**

Who cares about boring things like micrometers and pulleys and stainless steel rollers and industrial robotics? Some people do.

Our President should be mindful of the effort, experience, and background that it takes to keep an industrial society in motion and thriving. The word MICROMETER symbolizes some of the necessary, mysterious industrial makeup of our nation.

Tuesday, July 29, 2008

Poetic Word of the Day for Presidential Candidates: **DIPLOMATIC**

Here is another obvious word for our presidential candidates. The President, not just his Secretary of State, should be DIPLOMATIC. Diplomacy is wherever the President is. All of the people who work for the President should be DIPLOMATIC as well. And, believe it or not, this is a call for all citizens to become much more DIPLOMATIC. Maybe they should teach it in school. ALL of us should be DIPLOMATIC.

It is interesting that DIPLOMATIC sort of rhymes with "automatic" and "true fanatic."

Now, this is hard to grasp, but there are some people in our nation who don't believe in diplomacy at all.

Wednesday, July 30, 2008

Poetic Word of the Day for Presidential Candidates: **TEACHER**

We cannot underestimate the importance of a TEACHER in today's society. Our President as a TEACHER will teach us both the simple and the complex. He will read to grade school children and advise people on career options.

To put it simply, our President is our primary TEACHER. This is no easy task. He is intimate with the intricate educational system, and he teaches things that the educational system does not.

A President can teach the simple and the complex. He should have an understanding of the tough, hard sciences like chemistry as well as the social arts like psychology.

My grandfather once said to me, "Do you know when school is? ... Neither do I." This means that we never know when, or how, or where we just might learn something. "School" can be any time at all.

The presidential candidates should have a vision and a mission, and then be able to take us all somewhere together--not just rescue us from war and bail out the economy and prevent crises. A presidential candidate should always be reaching and digging further into what we need to be taught, like teaching us how to live well.

Thursday, July 31, 2008

Poetic Word of the Day for Presidential Candidates:
OUTDOORSMAN

A presidential candidate might be a rugged deer hunter, archer, fisherman, boater, golfer, ball player, jogger, rugby player, or a walker. He might be a skier or a motorcyclist! We hope he likes to do things outdoors, even if it is just the yardwork.

Friday, August 1, 2008

Poetic Word of the Day for Presidential Candidates: **LISTEN**

The message here is: Shut up and LISTEN! Knowing how to LISTEN is probably the best skill a presidential candidate can have.

Communication begins with listening. This is no joke. Oftentimes, we seem to know exactly what our best friend is going to say before the words come out of his/her mouth, but we still must shut up and LISTEN, even with our best friends.

That said, we hope the speeches are not too long unless the new President is going to teach us something. We do need some guiding speeches. We hope the issues aren't so numerous and problematic that we are denied some of the simple lessons and wisdom of a wise President.

How we talk and how we LISTEN make a huge difference in life. We definitely expect the President to have exceptional skills in listening.

Saturday, August 2, 2008

Poetic Word of the Day for Presidential Candidates: **ALCOHOLIC**

It's unfortunate, but we better have a President who knows well what alcoholism can do to a family. Strong men and women, even the grounded of our nation, can be ruined and can die from alcoholism--and they take their families down with them.

We can wish for a President who is not afraid of the hard problems like alcoholism, abortion, health care and Social Security. While we don't expect immediate results, we do expect results, and we're not afraid.

Sunday, August 3, 2008

Poetic Word of the Day for Presidential Candidates: **ASTRONAUT**

We are lucky to have a space program and double lucky that it is now cooperative between many nations. We hope our next President continues the support, both financially and in deep emotional spirit. Our astronauts and our space program might provide some kind of goal--a national long-term goal that gives all Americans a unifying, good reason to live.

Monday, August 4, 2008

Poetic Word of the Day for Presidential Candidates: **T-SHIRTS**

Americans love their T-SHIRTS. We can wear our cowboy shirts when we go to the rodeo, but our T-SHIRTS tell us who we are. My personal feeling is that making T-SHIRTS in the USA is a proud craft and good for our domestic economy.

The presidential candidates may have to dress up most of the time, but they should all still own a few T-SHIRTS.

Every day is National Wear Your T-SHIRT Day!

Tuesday, August 5, 2008

Poetic Word of the Day for Presidential Candidates: **HYDROGEN**

Teach us some science, Mr. President. Teach us about HYDROGEN. Is it true HYDROGEN is the most abundant element in the universe? Is HYDROGEN a chemical, a gas, or a fuel? Do astronauts use HYDROGEN in space? Teach us all about HYDROGEN, please Mr. President. There are many things to know about HYDROGEN. Could HYDROGEN science be the science that saves the planet from global warming?

Wednesday, August 6, 2008

Poetic Word of the Day for Presidential Candidates: **OCEAN LINERS**

OCEAN LINERS have millions of civilians on board, turn slowly, and require tug boat guides.

OCEAN LINERS are slow, smooth, and steady; and all of the passengers need stuff like food, refrigerators, ovens, cars, houses, school books, and to feel needed.

Maybe we can see some dolphins when we're out on the cruise!

Thursday, August 7, 2008

Poetic Word of the Day for Presidential Candidates: **HILLS**

We know there are HILLS on our ocean, Mr. President. There are grassy, green HILLS, and there are HILLS with abundant trees. There are HILLS with sparse trees and there are HILLS with horses grazing.

In Missouri we have "The HILLS of Oceola," a sweet song that boy scouts like to sing. In Austria (and in the movies), they have "The HILLS are Alive with the Sound of Music." HILLS are symbolic of the ups and downs of life that everyone will experience, perhaps even our nation as a whole will have many ups and downs. Nobody wishes to face the downs of life. It's hard and it takes more than hard work to get past them. What do we do when, and if, they come? Pray and face it--that's all I know. Pray and face the downs of life. Can life be all ups? I don't think so. Experience shows us that we will have downs, so we go through them. We pray that we won't have any more dust bowls and, certainly, we pray that we won't have any pestilence or epidemics in our world. We ask God the Father Almighty to help with these big unknowns. And, of course just because we are religious doesn't mean we ignore the science, (and then fail to make the correct choices that the farmers and agricultural scientists must make to avoid dust bowls and pestilence).

Friday, August 8, 2008

Poetic Word of the Day for Presidential Candidates: **FRIEND**

How simple a thought ... our new overriding philosophy should be to have friends. We need a FRIEND with whom to walk the hills. We need a FRIEND with whom to voyage the oceans. We need a FRIEND for our very weird/sick/strange, but harmless neighbor. People warn, "Stay away from that person. We don't want her around." She is just lonely and friendless because nobody seems to understand her. But we don't have to follow every word of her conversation.

Diplomats make friends all over the world, but it doesn't mean we must give millions and billions of dollars to all of those countries. If we face the truth, Mr. President, one can only have so many close friends because we've got to work. We've got to truck those miles and pilot those winds. That means that we don't have much time for friends. While we're working so much, we are giving you our time. We've got to trust you and believe in you--that you're making good, long-lasting, meaningful friendships. We can only hope and trust and believe in you and know that you and your mysterious business amigos, or so-called friends, won't lead us astray.

Saturday, August 9, 2008

Poetic Word of the Day for Presidential Candidates: **SKY**

The SKY is the limit of our love, Mr. President. The SKY is the limit of our love. If we need oil, let's get it with honey instead of bombs, Mr. President. Are we pretending?

With faith and confidence and belief and our products, we can buy the oil for the next 30 years while we master the new, necessary fuel cell technologies. In the meantime, we can make a peaceful attempt toward the desires of the people in the Middle East. How about we start to learn the languages of those countries?

Iran's official language is Persian. Iraq's official languages are Arabic and Kurdish. Assyrian and Turkmen are official languages in areas where the Assyrians and Iraqi Turkmen are located respectively; Armenian and Persian are also spoken, but to a lesser extent. If we really cared about keeping some peace in these regions we would be learning these languages.

Also, I hate to say it, but we better keep our eyes on North Korea. We should probably learn their language as well.

Sunday, August 10, 2008

Poetic Word of the Day for Presidential Candidates: **SIFT**

Will our new President be an effective realist? Even though a President is supposed to be generic and common, we still wish for an effective President. An effective President will not take on all issues, nor even be the spokesman for all issues. It seems that the effective realist part of the job description might be new. President Bush sure showed us that he thought the job description included taking on *all* issues.

This part is unknown: How does the President of 300 million people remain *effective*? Since there is such a cry for "no more politics as usual," how do you choose the issues to tackle? How do you delegate the rest of the issues to your friends and staff? Can we expect someone seeing reality as it is? Problem-solving on this order will take super-human effort.

How will you SIFT, Mr. President? Do you skim and scan the material? There is some danger to skimming and scanning-- missing some of the important facts. It could be helpful to have your staff skim with you to make sure you haven't missed anything. How will you SIFT? The obvious part about sifting, Mr. President, is that you have so, so much that you have to read. Typically, smart people learn how to read carefully and SIFT! This is both an art and a danger. SIFT carefully, Mr. President, SIFT carefully.

Monday, August 11, 2008

Poetic Word of the Day for Presidential Candidates: **HONORABLE**

A presidential candidate should have a giving, devout, benevolent, looks-out-for-you HONORABLE character.

This is one of the most difficult qualities to ask for, or expect, from a presidential candidate. In this day and age, it seems like screwing the government and screwing your fellow citizen is the norm. Honor seems to require super-human ability, so we are realistic and don't really expect it so much. But, that doesn't mean the President can mock and disrespect us with his actions by not looking out for the country's best interests.

Honor includes devotion and a giving personality. I don't think we are really getting anywhere because we're just throwing around high and mighty words, words that too easily fly out of our mouths as if someone really means them. Words have potential to shape our focus and our future and our character. Words can be so high and mighty . . . easily said but not so easily done.

Who knows? Maybe somewhere there are still some HONORABLE people left in this world. Let's take a look at ourselves for a moment. Even if we are past our formative years and we were not so HONORABLE back in those days, it doesn't mean we can't learn our lessons, take our spills, and become HONORABLE for the rest of our lives. It takes a lot of work. You have to encourage yourself and change yourself if you are prone to the kinds of mistakes that make one dishonorable. Remember, HONORABLE is way, way, way up there on the list of desirable qualities for human beings. How you handle things like "little white lies" is a big part of being HONORABLE. Of course, whether or not you participate in extramarital affairs is also one of the big things associated with being HONORABLE. So we, ourselves--the regular citizens, writers, teachers, and other workers--must attempt to be HONORABLE, if only to see how difficult it is and what, exactly, we are asking of our presidential candidates.

An HONORABLE President listens more than he speaks. We expect a President to be way more HONORABLE than we are. He should have lived a better, more HONORABLE life than all of us. That's not easy to do. McCain was a POW, and Obama is a lawyer. The lawyer has a chance at a cohesive, HONORABLE life lived; but most lawyers need someone with a problem (I guess), a problem that needs to go to court. I don't know about the HONORABLE, grounded life of a lawyer. It's been said that Obama gave time to people who needed assistance in Illinois, and we wonder if he's a good listener.

Tuesday, August 12, 2008

Poetic Word of the Day for Presidential Candidates: **INTRICATE**

How do politicians get INTRICATE?   INTRICATE seems to be a word for inventors and biochemistry researchers, not a word for politicians.

How about the presidential candidates get INTRICATE with the abortion doctors who need new jobs? How about they get INTRICATE with the weapons manufacturing employees who need new jobs? Exactly what I'm saying is that soon we won't need these professions anymore, so get INTRICATE and help these people find new careers. (Obviously, those of us who are concerned people are praying hard to end abortion, legal or not.)

Wednesday, August 13, 2008

Poetic Word of the Day for Presidential Candidates: **IMAGINE**

All of us can think, Mr. President, but you should be able to think and IMAGINE so fast that your superior ability sets you far apart from the rest of us. Even though you can think fast, can you collate all of the thinking? Can you keep it together? Can you examine all the sides of all the coins and stay open-minded to positions with which you may not initially agree? We are also depending on your nimble mind to provide a needed supply of comic relief, now and then.

You should also keep your thinking slowed to normal speed most of the time, so we can all work together toward the realization of fewer problems. How much "speed think" will you need to use? It is a good question. Remember, there is some danger to a fertile imagination. Sometimes we can go too far or IMAGINE things that have little practical application. Even

Thomas Edison and Albert Einstein worked on some maybe-not-so-practical projects in their later years. So, yes, we must be careful with our imagination too. However, usually, the more ideas that are presented for a solution to a particular problem, the better. Let's share our imaginations. That's how we more quickly learn whether or not we have a good idea.

Let's take a look at some possible good bumper stickers here: IMAGINE Peace … IMAGINE No Government … IMAGINE Free Energy … IMAGINE No Global Warming … IMAGINE Science … IMAGINE Jesus' House … IMAGINE No Politics As Usual … IMAGINE a Wise President … IMAGINE Solomon for President … IMAGINE a President who's not susceptible to Lobbyists.

Thursday, August 14, 2008

Poetic Word of the Day for Presidential Candidates: **SENSIBLE**

Being SENSIBLE means having common sense and being realistic. A presidential candidate may not have always had the fortunate life. He has probably had some adversity in life and knows the value of hard work.

We might appreciate our President not being afraid of doing some of his own research … in fact, a lot of it. Certainly, he will want assistance from his staff and advisors, but the President should be able to get the gist of the problem from his own research!

Believe it or not, a penny is still important to many people. Our President might wish to keep track of the pennies. Most of us don't know much about macroeconomics (if that's still what they call it these days). There's an old saying, "Watch out for the pennies and then the dollars will take care of themselves." There's another saying about being "penny wise and pound foolish." There are enough people on your payroll, Mr. President, that you can keep the dishonest purchases to a minimum. However, trillion dollar budgets are not easy to mind.

In the old days we heard about $500 hammers that the federal government had purchased. We don't wish to hear about anything like that again. How about this for a national goal: No more citizens will be cheating the government. Yes, that's looking backward. It's important, but let's also look forward.

Friday, August 15, 2008

Poetic Word of the Day for Presidential Candidates: **GRANDPA**

I loved my GRANDPA. We called him "Gramps." When we rode together in his truck, he'd slap his hand down on top of my hand, you know, in a loving and firm way. I remember his hand was very big. His elbows were big too. His love was never-ending. He helped all of his grandchildren. I loved the early mornings, when he liked to read the newspaper and drink a couple cups of coffee before he left for work. These are some of my fondest memories. When he retired, he still had the same coffee and newspaper routine early in the morning.

How can we ask and expect our President to be a GRANDPA to us? I don't know. We'll have to wait and see.

Saturday, August 16, 2008

Poetic Word of the Day for Presidential Candidates: **DEVOUT**

Please look up the definition of this word. It is exactly what we mean. We think a President should actively worship the Christian God (very sorry to the atheists and agnostics and gays, and those who believe in other gods). The message of Christianity is Jesus came to earth to save us and Yahweh is His Father. It takes work, self-evaluation, and self-correction to be Christian.

One line of the definition of DEVOUT from a dictionary: "Active in worship and prayer; religious."

Sunday, August 17, 2008

Poetic Word of the Day for Presidential Candidates: **COWBOY**

A COWBOY responds and mostly cooperates with "the establishment." COWBOYs are sensible, responsible, and hard-working, and independent.

So a President should not only be a connector, a diplomat, a salesperson, and a problem-solver, he should also be a COWBOY, independent and rugged. He should be willing and able to break from the establishment if necessary.

Monday, August 18, 2008

Poetic Word of the Day for Presidential Candidates: **TOUGH**

Get TOUGH and get real. Let's be TOUGH on ourselves and be courageous enough to ask ourselves how we address our pressing domestic issues, you know, the controversial money and life-and-death issues? Every time we start a war, there is less valuable time and attention spent on our TOUGH domestic issues.

We might ask for cautious and slow attention to tackle the TOUGH domestic issues over time without giving in to confusion and giving up. Some of these issues are abortion, weapons manufacturing and sales, health care, environmental issues, water issues, and Social Security issues.

Tuesday, August 19, 2008

Poetic Word of the Day for Presidential Candidates: **CAMPFIRE**

When you sit around the morning breakfast fire (CAMPFIRE with coffee) or evening CAMPFIRE with your buddies, you tell stories and sometimes you make things up. Well, that's when it's okay to be funny and stuff. But when you're the President, we need to know the truth. We expect a President to be honest. That's so obvious we should not even need to say it.   It is fundamentally essential that the President be an honest person, and we will check this out to every extreme. We will hold him to this standard every time.

Wednesday, August 20, 2008

Thank you for your interest in the *Poetic Word of the Day for Presidential Candidates*. There's quite a bit of wishful thinking in these poetic words.   There have been some impossible, unachievable ideals set forth, such as, we ask you to be *THOROUGH,* yet we expect you to *SIFT*. Those two poetic words don't interlock together so well.

This writing project is concluded now as the major ideas have been discussed.   Some of the other very obvious concepts we should examine such as *fiscal responsibility, commander in chief*, and *television (--managing the media--)* have been left out. It has been my hope that we could have several ideas to bounce around among our coffee teams at the campfire as we ponder our upcoming elections.

A few questions remain. For example, we'd like to know more about our fabric, what we are made of as Americans. Are we pursuing independent goals, or are we pursuing the goals of the crowd? Does money itself, as a tool, provide the necessary mechanisms of motivation overall in today's life in these United States, or shall we invent a new motivation tool? Will we ever know our limits?

We'd also like to know more about how competition enters into our political lives, good or bad, and who we are competing against. Is it the Russians, the Chinese, the French, the Mexicans, or mostly other Americans? And, what are we competing about … automobiles, economies, land and territory, space race, dominant personalities, or culture?

What is political competition? We don't know why political competition is ruining our country. Can we write another little booklet like this one and correct this deeply detrimental political competition that is pervading, seeping, permeating, saturating and is thoroughly ruining our country's politics?

These are questions for another day.

Here is the complete list of Poetic Words of the Day for Presidential Candidates:

Generic
Altruism
Thorough
Think
Grounded
Family
Reverent
Connector
Courageous
Coffee
Crisis
Crowd
Quarry
Tale
Sheriff
Athlete
Fast
Accept
Garden

Wheels
Aware
Fabric
Measured Change
Far
Pretend
Salvage
Actuator
Aquifer
Alpine
Rollers
Kindly
Micrometer
Diplomatic
Teacher
Outdoorsman
Listen
Alcoholic
Astronaut
T-Shirts
Hydrogen
Ocean Liners
Hills
Friend
Sky
Sift
Honorable
Intricate
Imagine
Sensible
Grandpa
Devout
Cowboy
Tough
Campfire

Very necessary and important poetic words of the day added later:

Eloquence
Depth
Optimism
Motivator
Risk
NASA
Renewal
Media Manager
Mourn
Made In USA

Another Day ...

Poetic Word of the Day for Presidential Candidates:
ELOQUENCE
The short definition of ELOQUENCE is "well said." One definition of ELOQUENCE is: Just the right kind of words put in the right place, and just the right amount of words. (Unfortunately, we find this word itself distasteful; however, it is probably necessary that we consider it). One of the important aspects of ELOQUENCE is being succinct. I do not believe that President Obama has been succinct. He talks too much and uses words that we do not understand. Those words are too big and are not what we call "straight talk." Oh, we are glad that he is so intelligent, but this is being inaccessible. We might ask: "Are these long-winded, befuddling speeches purposefully meant to be part of the confusion?"

Another Day ...
Poetic Word of the Day for Presidential Candidates: **DEPTH**
Having DEPTH does not mean that the presidential candidates must use big words beyond the understanding of most citizens. We can have DEPTH and still have "straight talk."

Another Day ...
Poetic Word of the Day for Presidential Candidates: **OPTIMISM**
We are asking that our presidential candidates spread the good words of OPTIMISM. We have plenty to look forward to in the future. There are plenty of things to be optimistic about.

Another Day ...
Poetic Word of the Day for Presidential Candidates: **MOTIVATOR**
This quality seems to be lacking. None of our leaders seem to inspire much motivation (well, maybe a little bit to encourage our schools to get better; but anybody can do that). We hope they think it is part of their jobs. We are not trying to just get legislation passed; we are trying to get somewhere.

Another Day ...
Poetic Word of the Day for Presidential Candidates: **RISK**
Yes, there may be a few, just a very few, times when our nation as a whole shall take a RISK. These instances will be few and far between ... as in this day and age, risk-taking is not in the usual best interest of this large ocean liner. However, I think it's a great thing to know and remember that it is on the table.

Another Day ...
Poetic Word of the Day for Presidential Candidates: **NASA**
We want a future. We want to get along with other nations, especially Russia and China. We want a quest! We want some great visions to hope for and to reach out for (not just consumerism and materialism). We want some national goals! You and I are not the only ones who are calling for national goals. We hope and pray that it is more than just feeding our faces and keeping a roof over our heads. Obviously, these basic needs should be addressed for those who don't have them, but there's probably not much of a solution for the poor and for those who do drugs and alcohol and lose everything. SEE? We want some national goals -- far reaching and complicated.

Another Day ...

Poetic Word of the Day for Presidential Candidates: **RENEWAL** SOMETHING ELSE--SO THAT PEOPLE WILL SOME DAY SOON HAVE THE GREATEST RESPECT FOR THE WHOLE POLITICAL SYSTEM--<u>RENEWAL</u> AND <u>RENEWED FAITH</u>. There was a time in the last few years when I was thinking that our whole nation should be broken up into three or four big parts so that people could begin again and develop a new national faith, a new era of accountability. Then I realized that the country is already broken up into 50 parts ... obviously, the 50 states. So, yes, we may already have our country broken into small enough pieces to be efficiently handled. But still, as we well know, the big federal government does not have our respect. This comment is just a point of view about the size of our nation. Is it small enough to manage? That's the question. It seems to me it is just common sense that anything that's *too big* can get away from you. It could be *too big to manage!* It could be as simple as that. This is a serious question that we must ask. We can ask these kinds of serious questions in our coffee gatherings and at our campfires.

Another Day ...

Poetic Word of the Day for Presidential Candidates: **MEDIA MANAGER**

The intent of this booklet is not to criticize the media. Although, we feel deeply that the media could be the single most influential factor that is contributing to the mistrust that people have for our government, especially the big federal government. Let's beware. Let's write another book about how the evening news, as it is now being presented on the major networks (CBS / ABC / NBC / PBS News Hour / FOX News / CNN / MSNBC), could definitely be going down the road that is leading to the loss of hope and creating much pessimism by the general public--all in the name of sensationalism and high ratings. It has been this way for years whether the media admits it or not. I think that we want to know about the "fleecing of America," but maybe, in this case, they should be more careful about the *way* they say it. The sensational tone that they use to present the news is subject. (Editor's note: "Less drama, more facts.")

Another Day ...
Poetic Word of the Day for Presidential Candidates: **MOURN**
CHIEF OF MOURNING AND CEREMONY FOR OUR DEAD

Another Day ...
Poetic Word of the Day for Presidential Candidates: **MADE IN USA**
Please, Mr. President, please work toward the acceptance of this deep desire that is residing and spreading in so many of us as United States citizens. We want to keep making things in America. We want to make our own stuff. We don't want globalism. Let us remind you that if we do any international trade, it's not to trade the things we need on an everyday basis. No, we don't want cars and T-shirts from international trade. We will accept international trade for items that are exotic and rare and original. These kinds of trade policies will serve our nation and our people best. No foreign soap, no foreign toothbrushes; no infinite varieties of toothpaste from Mexico, no foreign automatic dishwasher powder. NO. Yes, one-of-a-kind things like a Rolls Royce. Yes, bamboo, (all of bamboo used to come only from Asia). Yes, original artwork.

Of course, foreign nation artists could make designs for T-shirts and certain other products. Such designs could be considered original artwork. Then, perhaps, those designs could be sent to the U.S. and we can print and finish those T-shirts ourselves (on domestic cotton).

BONUS TEXT - Philosophical / Logical Proof for Following a Christian Way of Life
(The following is unedited, and not perfectly eloquent)
The following is one view; one approach as a logical position for the practicality and social applicability of following Christ and living a fully devout Christian life. This is a logical proof (to the best of my ability and understanding of logical proofs and symbolic logic language). It spells out the minimum reasoning

as to just how come that it makes the best sense to believe in Yahweh and follow Christianity.

Overview: Life is short. As time goes on, you'll probably prove that to yourself. Now, if we follow Christ and believe and choose to live a Christian way of life all of our days and expect to reach heaven at the end of life then we are **risking** that all of that is not really correct . . . And, risking not living a short lifetime of defined fun, hedonism, and/or egocentrically spreading one's genes – a possible aim of the "survival of the fittest" theories, observations, and behaviors. In short you might be risking having spent this life of Christianity in vein and missing a lot of certain kinds of fun.

So, I'm willing to risk a little bit of fun that I might have had and in turn devoutly believe in Jesus Christ the way to the Father. I don't take my short life that narcissistically serious. I'd much rather have a chance of gaining everlasting life in heaven than live for a little bit of sure fun on earth for a few years. In other words "survival of the fittest" pursuits are empty in the context of preparing for holy everlasting life.

The possible reward of everlasting life in heaven far outweighs the little bit of short lived pleasure, fun, and egocentrically spreading one's genes.

Christian rules: to follow the Christian rules makes for a better all-around world; as far as getting along with others and getting along with nations, and for more people living and spreading the wider greater good.

What we get: (the likely reality of) everlasting life.
What we risk: some kind of egocentric lifestyle; living totally for fun, pleasure, and perhaps one living to egocentrically spread one's genes.
What else we risk: that the living of life for fun, pleasure, and spreading one's genes may not provide good harmony living in with our fellow man.

What else we risk: coming to believe that there is no such thing as your guardian angel.

The greatest aim achievable (and the greatest aim by following Christ and the Holy Bible) is to reach everlasting heaven after we die. Remember: Heaven is supposed to be (defined as) some kind of great eternal everlasting (bliss) continuous, indescribable perfect joy.

The greatest result of living for now?? . . . living for pleasure in this world? You may get this fun, pleasure, and spread your genes; however then you die with no hope of everlasting life. Your time has ended and you die forever.

The simplified proof is something like this:

a = Life is temporary; the life we know from childhood to old age is fleeting and doesn't really last very long.

b = Living one's life to devoutly follow Jesus Christ and the Christian way of life.

c = Living one's life for selfish fun, selfish pleasure, and egocentrically spreading one's genes.

d = At the end of life there's the likely reality of making it to heaven (though the path is narrow and there's no guarantees).

e = dead forever.

If a, b, and not c, then d.
   or
If a, c, and not b, then e.

Either d or e is true. Not both.

Statement about studying the Holy Bible
Life must be a huge problem otherwise the Bible would not be such a big and intimidating book.

BONUS TEXT – CHAPTERS FROM THE BIBLE

In my humble opinion, I could never say anything better than the Bible says it. So, here are a few chapters of the Bible for you.

ISAIAH CHAPTERS 1 AND 2

1 The vision which Isaiah, son of Amoz, saw concerning Judah and Jerusalem in the days of Uzziah, Jotham, Ahaz and Hezekiah, kings of Judah.

ACCUSATION AND APPEAL

2* Hear, O heavens, and listen, O earth,
for the LORD speaks:
Sons have I raised and reared,
but they have rebelled against me![a]
3 An ox knows its owner,
and an ass, its master's manger;
But Israel does not know,
my people has not understood.[b]
4 Ah! Sinful nation, people laden with wickedness,
evil offspring, corrupt children!
They have forsaken the LORD,
spurned the Holy One of Israel,
apostatized,[c]
5 Why would you yet be struck,
that you continue to rebel?
The whole head is sick,
the whole heart faint.
6 From the sole of the foot to the head
there is no sound spot in it;
Just bruise and welt and oozing wound,
not drained, or bandaged,
or eased with salve.
7 Your country is waste,
your cities burnt with fire;
Your land—before your eyes
strangers devour it,
a waste, like the devastation of Sodom.[d]

8 And daughter Zion is left
like a hut in a vineyard,
Like a shed in a melon patch,
like a city blockaded.
9 If the LORD of hosts had not
left us a small remnant,
We would have become as Sodom,
would have resembled Gomorrah.
10 Hear the word of the LORD,
princes of Sodom!
Listen to the instruction of our God,
people of Gomorrah!
11 What do I care for the multitude of your sacrifices?
says the LORD.
I have had enough of whole-burnt rams
and fat of fatlings;
In the blood of calves, lambs, and goats
I find no pleasure.
12 When you come to appear before me,
who asks these things of you?
13 Trample my courts no more!
To bring offerings is useless;
incense is an abomination to me.
New moon and sabbath, calling assemblies—
festive convocations with wickedness—
these I cannot bear.
14 Your new moons and festivals I detest;
they weigh me down, I tire of the load.
15 When you spread out your hands,
I will close my eyes to you;
Though you pray the more,
I will not listen.
Your hands are full of blood!
16 Wash yourselves clean!
Put away your misdeeds from before my eyes;
cease doing evil;
17 learn to do good.
Make justice your aim: redress the wronged,
hear the orphan's plea, defend the widow.

18 Come now, let us set things right,
says the LORD:
Though your sins be like scarlet,
they may become white as snow;
Though they be red like crimson,
they may become white as wool.
19 If you are willing, and obey,
you shall eat the good things of the land;
20 But if you refuse and resist,
you shall be eaten by the sword:
for the mouth of the LORD has spoken!

THE PURIFICATION OF JERUSALEM

21 How she has become a prostitute,
the faithful city, so upright!
Justice used to lodge within her,
but now, murderers.
22 Your silver is turned to dross,
your wine is mixed with water.
23 Your princes are rebels
and comrades of thieves;
Each one of them loves a bribe
and looks for gifts.
The fatherless they do not defend,
the widow's plea does not reach them.
24 Now, therefore, says the Lord,
the LORD of hosts, the Mighty One of Israel:
Ah! I will take vengeance on my foes
and fully repay my enemies!
25 I will turn my hand against you,
and refine your dross in the furnace,
removing all your alloy.
26 I will restore your judges as at first,
and your counselors as in the beginning;
After that you shall be called
city of justice, faithful city.
27 Zion shall be redeemed by justice,
and her repentant ones by righteousness.
28 Rebels and sinners together shall be crushed,
those who desert the LORD shall be consumed.

JUDGMENT ON THE SACRED GROVES

29 You shall be ashamed of the terebinths which you desired,
and blush on account of the gardens which you chose.
30 You shall become like a terebinth whose leaves wither,
like a garden that has no water.
31 The strong tree shall turn to tinder,
and the one who tends it shall become a spark;
Both of them shall burn together,
and there shall be none to quench them.

CHAPTER 2

1 This is what Isaiah, son of Amoz, saw concerning Judah and Jerusalem.

ZION, THE ROYAL CITY OF GOD

2 In days to come,
The mountain of the LORD's house
shall be established as the highest mountain
and raised above the hills.
All nations shall stream toward it.ᵃ
3 Many peoples shall come and say:
"Come, let us go up to the LORD's mountain,
to the house of the God of Jacob,
That he may instruct us in his ways,
and we may walk in his paths."ᵇ
For from Zion shall go forth instruction,
and the word of the LORD from Jerusalem.
4 He shall judge between the nations,
and set terms for many peoples.
They shall beat their swords into plowshares
and their spears into pruning hooks;ᶜ
One nation shall not raise the sword against another,
nor shall they train for war again.ᵈ
5 House of Jacob, come,
let us walk in the light of the LORD!

THE LORD'S DAY OF JUDGMENT ON PRIDE

6 You have abandoned your people,
the house of Jacob!
Because they are filled with diviners,

and soothsayers, like the Philistines;
with foreigners they clasp hands.[e]
7 Their land is full of silver and gold,
there is no end to their treasures;
Their land is full of horses,
there is no end to their chariots.
8 Their land is full of idols;
they bow down to the works of their hands,
what their fingers have made.[f]
9 So all shall be abased,
each one brought low.
Do not pardon them!
10 Get behind the rocks,
hide in the dust,
From the terror of the LORD
and the splendor of his majesty!
11 The eyes of human pride shall be lowered,
the arrogance of mortals shall be abased,
and the LORD alone will be exalted, on that day.
12 For the LORD of hosts will have his day
against all that is proud and arrogant,
against all that is high, and it will be brought low;
13 Yes, against all the cedars of Lebanon
and against all the oaks of Bashan,
14 Against all the lofty mountains
and all the high hills,
15 Against every lofty tower
and every fortified wall,
16 Against all the ships of Tarshish
and all stately vessels.

17 Then human pride shall be abased,
the arrogance of mortals brought low,
And the LORD alone will be exalted on that day.
18 The idols will vanish completely.
19 People will go into caves in the rocks
and into holes in the earth,
At the terror of the LORD
and the splendor of his majesty,

as he rises to overawe the earth.
20 On that day people shall throw to moles and bats
their idols of silver and their idols of gold
which they made for themselves to worship.
21 And they shall go into caverns in the rocks
and into crevices in the cliffs,
At the terror of the LORD
and the splendor of his majesty,
as he rises to overawe the earth.
22   As for you, stop worrying about mortals,
in whose nostrils is but a breath;
for of what worth are they?

SIRACH CHAPTERS 24-26

PRAISE OF WISDOM

1   Wisdom sings her own praises,
among her own people she proclaims her glory.
2   In the assembly of the Most High she opens her mouth,
in the presence of his host she tells of her glory:
3   "From the mouth of the Most High I came forth,
and covered the earth like a mist.
4   In the heights of heaven I dwelt,
and my throne was in a pillar of cloud.
5   The vault of heaven I compassed alone,
and walked through the deep abyss.
6   Over waves of the sea, over all the land,
over every people and nation I held sway.
7   Among all these I sought a resting place.
In whose inheritance should I abide?
8   "Then the Creator of all gave me his command,
and my Creator chose the spot for my tent.
He said, 'In Jacob make your dwelling,
in Israel your inheritance.'
9   Before all ages, from the beginning, he created me,
and through all ages I shall not cease to be.
10   In the holy tent I ministered before him,
and so I was established in Zion.

11 In the city he loves as he loves me, he gave me rest;
in Jerusalem, my domain.
12 I struck root among the glorious people,
in the portion of the Lord, his heritage.
13 "Like a cedar in Lebanon I grew tall,
like a cypress on Mount Hermon;
14 I grew tall like a palm tree in Engedi,
like rosebushes in Jericho;
Like a fair olive tree in the field,
like a plane tree beside water I grew tall.
15 Like cinnamon and fragrant cane,
like precious myrrh I gave forth perfume;
Like galbanum and onycha and mastic,[b]
like the odor of incense in the holy tent.
16 "I spread out my branches like a terebinth,
my branches so glorious and so graceful.
17 I bud forth delights like a vine;
my blossoms are glorious and rich fruit.[†]
19 Come to me, all who desire me,
and be filled with my fruits.
20 You will remember me as sweeter than honey,
better to have than the honeycomb.
21 Those who eat of me will hunger still,
those who drink of me will thirst for more.[c]
22 Whoever obeys me will not be put to shame,
and those who serve me will never go astray."
23 All this is the book of the covenant of the Most High God,[d]
the Law which Moses commanded us
as a heritage for the community of Jacob.[†]
25 It overflows, like the Pishon, with wisdom,[e]
and like the Tigris at the time of first fruits.
26 It runs over, like the Euphrates, with understanding,
and like the Jordan at harvest time.
27 It floods like the Nile with instruction,
like the Gihon at vintage time.
28 The first human being never finished comprehending wisdom,
nor will the last succeed in fathoming her.
29 For deeper than the sea are her thoughts,

and her counsels, than the great abyss.
30   Now I, like a stream from a river,
and like water channeling into a garden—
31   I said, "I will water my plants,
I will drench my flower beds."
Then suddenly this stream of mine became a river,
and this river of mine became a sea.
32   Again I will make my teachings shine forth like the dawn;
I will spread their brightness afar off.
33   Again I will pour out instruction like prophecy
and bestow it on generations yet to come.

Chapter 25

THOSE WHO ARE WORTHY OF PRAISE
1   With three things I am delighted,
for they are pleasing to the Lord and to human beings:
Harmony among relatives, friendship among neighbors,
and a wife and a husband living happily together.
2   Three kinds of people I hate,
and I loathe their manner of life:
A proud pauper, a rich liar,
and a lecherous old fool.
3   In your youth you did not gather.
How will you find anything in your old age?
4   How appropriate is sound judgment in the gray-haired,
and good counsel in the elderly!
5   How appropriate is wisdom in the aged,
understanding and counsel in the venerable!
6   The crown of the elderly, wide experience;
their glory, the fear of the Lord.
7   There are nine who come to mind as blessed,
a tenth whom my tongue proclaims:
The man who finds joy in his children,
and the one who lives to see the downfall of his enemies.
8   Happy the man who lives with a sensible woman,
and the one who does not plow with an ox and a donkey combined.

Happy the one who does not sin with the tongue,
who does not serve an inferior.
9   Happy the one who finds a friend,
who speaks to attentive ears.
10   How great is the one who finds wisdom,
but none is greater than the one who fears the Lord.
11   Fear of the Lord surpasses all else.
To whom can we compare the one who has it?

WICKED AND VIRTUOUS WOMEN

13   Any wound, but not a wound of the heart!
Any wickedness, but not the wickedness of a woman!
14   Any suffering, but not suffering from one's foes!
Any vengeance, but not the vengeance of one's enemies!
15   There is no poison worse than that of a serpent,
no venom greater than that of a woman.
16   I would rather live with a dragon or a lion
than live with a wicked woman.[a]
17   A woman's wicked disposition changes her appearance,
and makes her face as dark as a bear.
18   When her husband sits among his neighbors,
a bitter sigh escapes him unawares.
19   There is hardly an evil like that in a woman;
may she fall to the lot of the sinner!
20   Like a sandy hill to aged feet
is a garrulous wife to a quiet husband.
21   Do not be enticed by a woman's beauty,
or be greedy for her wealth.
22   Harsh is the slavery and great the shame
when a wife supports her husband.
23   Depressed mind, gloomy face,
and a wounded heart—a wicked woman.
Drooping hands and quaking knees,
any wife who does not make her husband happy.
24   With a woman sin had a beginning,
and because of her we all die.
25   Allow water no outlet,
and no boldness of speech to a wicked woman.
26   If she does not go along as you direct,
cut her away from you.

Chapter 26

1   Happy the husband of a good wife;
the number of his days will be doubled.[a]
2   A loyal wife brings joy to her husband,
and he will finish his years in peace.
3   A good wife is a generous gift
bestowed upon him who fears the Lord.[b]
4   Whether rich or poor, his heart is content,
a smile ever on his face.
5   There are three things I dread,
and a fourth which terrifies me:
Public slander, the gathering of a mob,
and false accusation—all harder to bear than death.
6   A wife jealous of another wife is heartache and mourning;
everyone feels the lash of her tongue.
7   A wicked wife is a chafing yoke;
taking hold of her is like grasping a scorpion.
8   A drunken wife arouses great anger,
for she does not hide her shame.
9   By her haughty stare and her eyelids
an unchaste wife can be recognized.
10   Keep a strict watch over an unruly wife,
lest, finding an opportunity, she use it;[c]
11   Watch out for her impudent eye,
and do not be surprised if she betrays you:
12   As a thirsty traveler opens his mouth
and drinks from any water nearby,
So she sits down before every tent peg
and opens her quiver for every arrow.
13   A gracious wife delights her husband;
her thoughtfulness puts flesh on his bones.
14   A silent wife is a gift from the Lord;
nothing is worth more than her self-discipline.
15   A modest wife is a supreme blessing;
no scales can weigh the worth of her chastity.
16   The sun rising in the Lord's heavens—
the beauty of a good wife in her well-ordered home.
17   The light which shines above the holy lampstand—

a beautiful face on a stately figure.
18   Golden columns on silver bases—
so her shapely legs and steady feet.

DANGERS TO INTEGRITY AND FRIENDSHIP
28   Two things bring grief to my heart,
and a third arouses my anger:
The wealthy reduced to want,
the intelligent held in contempt,
And those who pass from righteousness to sin—
the Lord prepares them for the sword.
29   A merchant can hardly keep from wrongdoing,
nor can a shopkeeper stay free from sin;

We wish to thank our editors: Dawn Vandendaele Sparks and Carol G. Elkins.
We wish to thank our cover artist.

Contact Information:
Mr. and Mrs. Paul Christopher Anzalone
Kansas City, Missouri, USA
RICHARD.HOEDL@GMAIL.COM
816-682-2068

Also known online as MissouriRick / ChristianPolarBear / PolarBear / MathBear / Richard Hoedl / Anzo / AnzoMaslow / Visit a kind music Blog: www.AnzoMaslow.Blogspot.com / Visit a kind YouTube channel: No Nonsense Forgotten Pop.

Many interests: Music, Clean Energy, Nuclear Disarmament, Chess, Anti-Abortion hopes, Alternatives to the Death Penalty hopes, Repeal Daylight Savings Time hopes, Space Program, Nonsense Poetry for children and adults, Middle School Math Tutor and Volunteer, Christianity and Catholicism.